For my father Robin

Text copyright © 1961 by James Reeves
Illustrations copyright © 1990 by Emma Chichester Clark
All rights reserved. No part of this book may be reproduced in any form
or by any electronic or mechanical means, including information storage
and retrieval systems, without permission in writing from the publisher,
except by a reviewer who may quote brief passages in a review.
First U.S. edition 1990
First published in Great Britain in 1990
by Walker Books Ltd.

Library of Congress Cataloging-in-Publication Data

Reeves, James.
Ragged Robin: poems from A to Z / by James Reeves;
pictures by Emma Chichester Clark. – 1st U.S. ed.
p.   cm.
"First published in Great Britain in 1990
by Walker Books Ltd." – Verso t.p.
Summary: Nonsense verses, ballads, and other poems on a magical theme
introduce the letters of the alphabet, from King Arthur in Avalon
through Moths and Moonshine to Zachary Zed.
ISBN 0-316-73829-8
1. Children's poetry, English. [1. English poetry.
2. Alphabet.] I. Clark, Emma Chichester, ill. II. Title.
PR6035.E38R34 1990.
821'.912-dc20
[E]   89-39450
                                        CIP
                                        AC

10   9   8   7   6   5   4   3   2   1

Published simultaneously in Canada
by Little, Brown & Company (Canada) Limited.

Printed in Italy

Ragged Robin

Poems from A to Z by James Reeves

Pictures by Emma Chichester Clark

Little, Brown and Company
Boston Toronto London

Ragged Robin

Robin was a king of men,
A king of far renown,
But then he fell on evil days
And lost his royal crown.
Ragged Robin he was called;
He lived in ragged times,
And so to earn his livelihood
He took to making rhymes.

A score or so of ragged rhymes
He made – some good, some bad;
He sang them up and down the lanes
Till people called him mad.
They listened for Mad Robin's songs
Through all the countryside,
And when they heard his voice no more
They guessed that he had died.

Now Ragged Robin was not dead
But changed into a bird,
And every year on tile and tree
His piping voice is heard.
His breast is clad with scarlet red,
His cloak and hood are brown;
And once more he is Winter's king
Although he wears no crown.

Cold are the skies where Robin reigns,
And evergreen his throne.
He whistles to defy the wind;
His tunes are all his own.
But here within this book are set
Some of the ragged rhymes
Mad Robin by the hedgerows sang
In far-off ragged times.

Twenty-six Letters

Twenty-six cards in half a pack;
Twenty-six weeks in half a year;
Twenty-six letters dressed in black
In all the words you ever will hear.

In "King," "Queen," "Ace," and "Jack,"
In "London," "lucky," "lone," and "lack,"
"January," "April," "forty," "fix,"
You'll never find more than twenty-six.

Think of the beautiful things you see
On mountain, riverside, meadow and tree.
How many their names are, but how small
The twenty-six letters that spell them all.

A
Avalon

In Avalon lies Arthur yonder;
Over his head the planets wander.
    A great King
    And a great King was he.

By his side sleeps Guinevere;
Of ladies she had no peer.
    A fair Queen
    And a fair Queen was she.

At midnight comes Jack the Knave
By moonlight to rob their grave.
    A false boy
    And a false boy is he.

Jewels he takes, and rings,
The gift of nobles and kings –
    Bright things,
    O bright things to see!

On harvest-field and town
The moon and stars look down.
Centuries without number
King and Queen are a-slumber.
    Long have they lain.
In time they will rise again
And all false knaves be slain.
Once more Arthur shall reign.
    A great King
    And a great King is he.

B

Brand the Blacksmith

Brand the Blacksmith with his hard hammer
Beats out shoes for the hooves of horses.
Bagot the Boy works at the bellows
To make fine mounts for the King's forces.

Better the music than bell or bugle
When "Huff!" go the bellows and "Ding!" goes the hammer.
"Better this work by far," says Bagot,
"Than banging of school bell and grinding at grammar."

C

Castles and Candlelight

Castles and candlelight
Are courtly things.
Turreted high
For the children of Kings
Stands the fair castle
Over the strand,
And there with a candle
In her thin hand,
With tunes in her ears
And gold on her head
Climbs the sad Princess
Upstairs to bed.

Castles and candlelight
Are cruel things,
For castles have dungeons,
And moths have wings.
Woe to the shepherd-boy
Who in darkness lies,
For viewing the Princess
With love in his eyes.
Ah, the poor shepherd-boy –
How long will it be
Before the proud King
Will let him go free?

D

The Song of D

Who will sing me the song of D?
How many dancers can you see?
Dinah, Deborah, Duncan, Dick,
And Dan with his fiddle and fiddling stick.
    Sing it low, sing it high,
Till the glory shines in the western sky.

Who will sing me the song of D?
How many cities can you see?
From Dublin Town we'll all jump over
To Dartmouth, Darlington, Deal and Dover.
    Sing it low, sing it high,
Till the glory shines in the western sky.

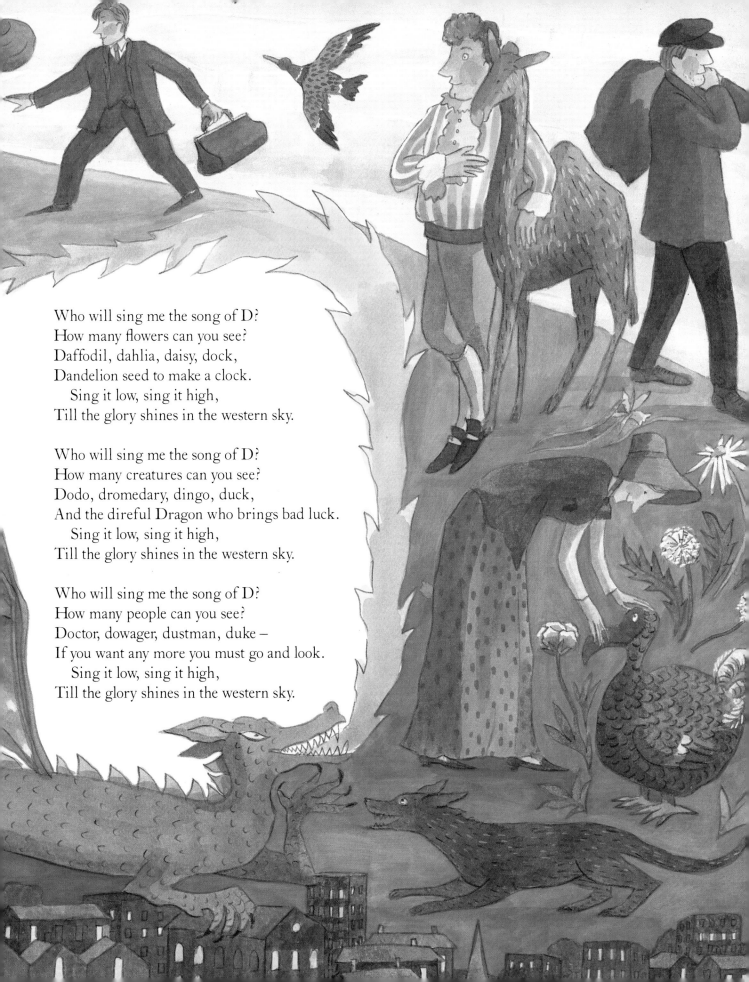

Who will sing me the song of D?
How many flowers can you see?
Daffodil, dahlia, daisy, dock,
Dandelion seed to make a clock.
    Sing it low, sing it high,
Till the glory shines in the western sky.

Who will sing me the song of D?
How many creatures can you see?
Dodo, dromedary, dingo, duck,
And the direful Dragon who brings bad luck.
    Sing it low, sing it high,
Till the glory shines in the western sky.

Who will sing me the song of D?
How many people can you see?
Doctor, dowager, dustman, duke –
If you want any more you must go and look.
    Sing it low, sing it high,
Till the glory shines in the western sky.

Egg to Eat

Early this morning when earth was empty
I went to the farmyard to fetch me an egg.
I spoke to the pullets who strolled about scratching
And the proud feathered cock who stood on one leg.

"Not an egg! Not an egg!" they all said together.
"We haven't been given any corn for two days."
So I went to the merchant who lives by the market,
And I asked him to give me some barley and maize.

"Not a grain! Not a grain!" was the corn-merchant's
    answer.
"I need a new wheel for to fix on my cart."
So I said to the wheelwright, "Please give me a wheel, sir,
For without it the corn-merchant's wagon won't start."

"Not a wheel, not a wheel can I make!" said the
    wheelwright.
"If you bring a new hammer, why then I will try."
So I searched up and down, but I couldn't find a hammer,
And I went to the forest to sit down and cry.

There I met an old wife and asked her politely,
"Oh madam, can you lend me a hammer, I beg?"
"Why no," said the wife, "for I haven't got a hammer,
But if it will help you, I will give you an egg."

So she gave me an egg, and I said to her, "Madam,
This surely must be the best egg ever born."
"So it is," said the wife. "If you want the best eggs,
You must always give your laying birds plenty of corn."

F

Flowers and Frost

Flowers are yellow
And flowers are red;
Frost is white
As an old man's head.
Daffodil, foxglove,
Rose, sweet pea –
Flowers and frost
Can never agree.
Flowers will wither
And summer's lost
When over the mountain
Comes King Frost.

White are the fields
Where King Frost reigns;
And the ferns he draws
On window-panes,
White and stiff
Are their curling fronds.

White are the hedges
And stiff are the ponds.
So cruel and hard
Is winter's King,
With his icy breath
On everything.

Then up comes the sun;
Down fall the showers.
Welcome to spring
And her yellow flowers!
So sing the birds
On the budding tree,
For frost and flowers
Can never agree;
And welcome, sunshine,
That we may say
The old cruel King
Is driven away.

G

Green Grass

Green grass is all I hear
And grass is all I see
When through tall fields I wander
Swish-swishing to the knee.

Grass is short on the high heath
And long on the hillside.
There's where the rabbits burrow,
And here's where I hide.

The hillside is my castle,
Its walls are the tall grass;
Over them I peer and pry
To see the people pass.

Long and far I send my gaze
Over the valleys low.
There I can see but do not hear
The wagons lumbering slow.

Horseman, footman, shepherd, dog –
Here in my castle green
I see them move through vale and village,
I see but am not seen.

Green grasses whispering round me,
All in the summer fine,
Tell me your secrets, meadow grasses,
And I will tell you mine.

H
Heroes on Horseback

Heroes on horseback
Hunt in their hundreds,
Leaving their halls
In the hurry of morn.
High on the hilltop
Is heard the thunder
Of hooves, and the hue
Of hound and horn.

Here in their homesteads
Hover the housewives,
Baking and brewing
Or busy with brush.
Gaily they gossip
And stitch for the children;
For hunting and harrying
They care not a rush.

High in the heavens
The hooked moon hangs.
Home come the hunters
Hungry as hawks.
Never a hare
Has Harry the Huntsman
Caught the whole day,
But hark how he talks!

"Hunters on horseback
Are braggers and boasters!"
So say the housewives
Who give them their stew.
"Without us women
To work and wait on them
What would these heroes,
Our husbands, do?"

I
Islands

I, with my mind's eye, see
Islands and indies fair and free,
Fair and far in the coral sea.

Out of the sea rise palmy shores;
Out of the shore rise plumy trees;
Out of each tree a feathered bird
   Sings with a voice like which
      no voice was ever heard,
And palm and plume and feather
Blend and bloom together
In colors like the green
      of summer weather.

And in this island scene
There is no clash nor quarrel;
Here the seas wash
In shining fields of coral
Indies and isles that lie
Deep in my mind's eye.

J

Jargon

Jerusalem, Joppa, Jericho –
These are the cities of long ago.

Jasper, jacinth, jet and jade –
Of such are jewels for ladies made.

Juniper's green and jasmine's white,
Sweet jonquil is spring's delight.

Joseph, Jeremy, Jennifer, James,
Julian, Juliet – just names.

January, July and June –
Birthday late or birthday soon.

Jacket, jersey, jerkin, jeans —
What's the wear for sweet sixteens?

Jaguar, jackal, jumbo, jay —
Came to dinner but couldn't stay.

Jellies, junkets, jumbles, jam —
Mix them up for sweet-toothed Sam.

To jig, to jaunt, to jostle, to jest —
These are the things that Jack loves best.

Jazz, jamboree, jubilee, joke —
The jolliest words you ever spoke.

From A to Z and Z to A
The joyfullest letter of all is J.

K

Kay

Kay, Kay,
Good Sir Kay,
Lock the gate
Till dawn of day,
So to keep bad men away.

This is the Keep,
And this is the key.
Who keeps the key
Of the Keep?
         Sir Kay.

Kay, Kay,
Good Sir Kay,
Lock the gate
Till dawn of day.

The bell has rung
To evensong.
The priest has blessed
The kneeling throng.
In bower and hall
To bed have gone
Knights and squires
All and one,
Lords and ladies
One and all,
Groom in kitchen,
Steed in stall.

Kay, Kay,
Good Sir Kay,
Lock the gate
Till dawn of day.

On shield and scabbard
Starlight falls,
Stalk the watchmen
Along the walls.
From hazel thicket
The screech-owl calls.
By the dying fire
The boarhounds sleep.
Sir Kay, Sir Kay,
Lock fast the Keep.

This is the Keep,
And this is the key.
Who keeps the key
Of the Keep?
         Sir Kay.

Kay, Kay,
Good Sir Kay,
Lock the gate
Till dawn of day,
So to keep bad men away.

It is late, late.
Lock fast the gate.

L
Long

A short word and a short word is "long,"
So let's have a short, not a long song.

   "Long was my beard," said the sailor,
     "Before we reached port."
   "Long are my dreams," said the old man,
     "But memory's short."
   "Long are all days," said the children,
     "With few of them gone."
   "Long are all lanes," said the wanderer,
     "Leading me on."

A short word and a short word is "long,"
So let's have a short, not a long song.

The sailor mended his tackle
   And searched for a breeze.
The old man thought of a voyage
   To unmapped seas.
The children, weary of playing,
   Came from the green;
The wanderer sighed for a home
   He had never seen.

A short word and a short word is "long,"
So that was a short, not a long song.

M
Moths and Moonshine

Moths and moonshine mean to me
Magic – madness – mystery.

Witches dancing weird and wild
Mischief make for man and child.

Owls screech from woodland shades,
Moths glide through moonlit glades,

Moving in dark and secret wise
Like a plotter in disguise.

Moths and moonshine mean to me
Magic – madness – mystery.

N

Noah

Noah was an Admiral;
Never a one but he
Sailed for forty days and nights
With wife and children three
On such a mighty sea.

Under his tempest-battered deck
This Admiral had a zoo;
And all the creatures in the world,
He kept them, two by two –
Ant, hippo, kangaroo,
And every other beast beside,
Of every mold and make.
When tempests howled and thunder growled
How they did cower and quake
To feel the vessel shake!

But Noah was a Carpenter
Had made his ship so sound
That not a soul of crew or zoo
In all that time was drowned
Before they reached dry ground.

So Admiral, Keeper, Carpenter –
Now should *you* put to sea
In such a flood, it would be good
If one of these you be,
But better still – all three!

O

O Nay!

"O nay! O nay! O nay!"
I heard the crier call.
"There is no news today –
No news, no news at all.

"No cow has gone astray!"
I heard the crier call.
"No foe is on the way!
There is no news at all.

"The Mayor has gone away.
  Good people, one and all,
Are now on holiday,"
  I heard the crier call.

"O nay! O nay! O nay!"
  I heard the crier cry.
"No folks in town do stay –
  Methinks no more will I!"

P aper

Paper makes a picture book;
Paper and a pin
Make a colored parcel
To wrap a present in.

Paper makes a letter
That makes a lady sad;
And sometimes it makes money
To make a poor man glad.

Paper, paper, paper
Makes a lawyer's clerk
Scribble, scratch and scribble
From morn till dead of dark.

Paper makes a dunce's cap;
Paper makes a kite.
I watch it rise upon the wind
And vanish out of sight.

Paper makes all shapes of things;
But best of all to me,
A paper boat upon the stream
Goes bobbing off to sea.

Quiet

Of all creatures
    Quiet is the shyest;
She has her finger to her lips.
She loves not cities
    but a mountain lakeside
Where peaceful water laps.

At nesting-time
    to see the mother blackbird
Quiet on tiptoe creeps;
And in the kitchen
    with scarce a blink she watches
The mice come out for scraps.

In fairgrounds
    or by the August seaside
Quiet will not stop;
But walks in winter
    on snow fresh-fallen
With light and muffled step.

She loves the fireside
    when the guests have gone,
And downward the ember slips;
Beside the cot she lingers
    hardly breathing
Because the baby sleeps.

R

Rain

Rain and rain is all I see
Falling on roof and stone and tree,
And all I hear is rain and rain
Hush-hushing on lawn and lane.

Moor and meadow, fern and flower
Drink the raindrops, hour by hour.
How sparkling are the ivy leaves
That catch the drops from farmhouse eaves!

When in my attic bed I lie
I hear it fall from the cloudy sky,
Hush-hushing all around
With its low and lulling sound.

Then in the light of morning clear
How new and green all things appear;
Then flow the brooks, and springs the grain,
And birds give joyful thanks for rain.

Rain, rain no more I hear,
But only bird-songs everywhere;
And rain, rain no more I see,
But shining sun on roof and tree.

S

Sky, Sea, Shore

Stars in a frosty sky
Crackle and blaze;
Streams in the lowland meadows
Linger and laze;
Shells on the seashore gleam,
Washed by the tide;
Seagulls over the harbor
Circle and glide.
   Blue smoke and prancing steed,
   Swallow and snake and swan –
   How many more
   Curving, glistening S-things
   In sky, sea, shore?

Tarlingwell

A town of ten towers
Is Tarlingwell,
And in every tower
There hangs a bell.

At twelve by the clock
What a ding-dang-dell
Sounds from the towers
Of Tarlingwell!

Over the broad
And blustery weald
So many voices
Never pealed.

Harsh or mellow,
Cracked or sound,
They tell the people
For miles around

That Tarlingwell
With its ten towers tall
Still stands, whatever
Else may fall.

U
Un

Uncut is your corn, Farmer Hearn,
Unstacked your hay.
Unfed, your fifteen pigs
Have run away.

Unpaid are your men, Farmer Hearn,
Unpainted your byre.
Unswept is your kitchen floor,
Unlit your fire.

Unmade is your bed, Farmer Hearn,
Uncombed your hair;
You have gone with the gypsy-men
Off to the fair.

Fiddling and sing-song, Farmer Hearn,
They're the ruin of you.
When unkind winter blows
What will you do?

V

Vain

Vain is the Princess Vara,
    Her mother's eldest daughter.
She looks all day in the mirror
    As a swan in the smooth water.

Her eyes are blue like the waves,
    Her skin is soft and fair;
Red-gold like the autumn leaves
    And thick and long is her hair.

And all for her pride and beauty,
   Gold hair and eyes of blue,
From far-off court and city
   The young men come to woo.

But to none will she answer Yes,
   For none but herself loves she,
Gazing all day in the glass
   With her eyes like the lonely sea.

W
Words

In woods are words.
You hear them all,
Winsome, witless or wise,
When the birds call.

In woods are words.
If your ears wake
You hear them, quiet and clear,
When the leaves shake.

In woods are words.
You hear them all
Blown by the wet wind
When raindrops fall.

In woods are words
Kind or unkind;
Birds, leaves and hushing rain
Bring them to mind.

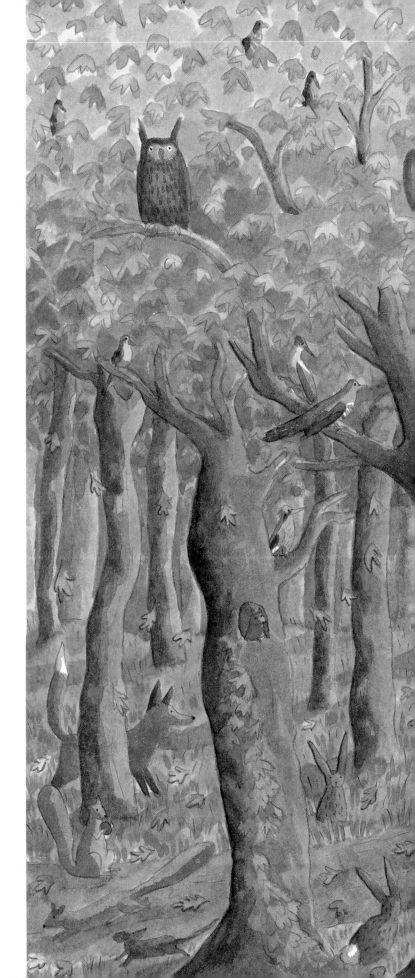

X

X-roads

Beside the cross-roads on the hill
With crossed sails stands the mill
    That once ground corn to make men bread.
Up to that hill two armies came
With crossed swords to fight for fame.
    Night fell on many brave men dead.

These are the words the four winds cried:
"Fame is a shadow: vain is pride;
    Trampled cornfields will not grow."
Now if those men had ceased from strife
And harkened to the winds of life,
    They would have lived to plow and sow.

Y
Yonder

Through yonder park there runs a stream;
By yonder stream there sits a man;
As yonder man in silence sits
He catches fish as best he can.

While yonder fish, one, two and three,
Through yonder limpid waters steer,
Why does yon silent fisherman
Drop first a sigh and then a tear?

Why does he cast yon fishing-line
Again, again, and all for nought?
It is because yon little fish,
For all his care, will *not* be caught.

Z

Zachary Zed

Zachary Zed was the last man,
 The last man left on earth.
For everyone else had died but him
 And no more come to birth.

In former times young Zachary
 Had asked a maid to wed.
"I loves thee, dear," he told her true,
 "Will thou be Missus Zed?"

"No, not if you was the last man
 On earth!" the maid replied:
And he was; but she wouldn't give consent,
 And in due time she died.

So all alone stood Zachary.
    "'Tis not so bad," he said,
"There's no one to make me brush my hair
    Nor send me up to bed.

"There's none can call me wicked,
    Nor none to argufy,
So dang my soul if I don't per-nounce
    LONG LIVE KING ZACHAR-Y!"

So Zachary Zed was the last man
    And the last King beside,
And never a person lived to tell
    If ever Zachary died.